★ *GREAT SPORTS TEAMS* ★

THE BOSTON

BASEBALL TEAM

John Grabowski

Enslow Publishers, Inc.

40 Industrial Road   PO Box 38
Box 398   Aldershot
Berkeley Heights, NJ 07922   Hants GU12 6BP
USA   UK

http://www.enslow.com

Library of Congress Cataloging-in-Publication Data

Grabowski, John F.
    The Boston Red Sox baseball team / John Grabowski.
        p. cm. (Great sports teams)
    Includes bibliographical references and index.
    Summary: Surveys the history of the legendary Boston Red Sox, covering
some of their key players and coaches and some of the best games the team
has played.
    ISBN 0-7660-1488-6
    1. Boston Red Sox (Baseball team)–History–Juvenile literature. [1. Boston
Red Sox (Baseball team)–History. 2. Baseball–History.] I. Title. II. Series
GV875.G73 2001
796.357'64'0974461–dc21
                                                                00-009111

Printed in the United States of America

10 9 8 7 6 5 4 3 2 1

To Our Readers: All Internet Addresses in this book were active and appropriate
when we went to press. Any comments or suggestions can be sent by e-mail to
Comments@enslow.com or to the address on the back cover.

Illustration Credits: AP/Wide World Photos

Cover Illustration: AP/Wide World Photos

Cover Description: Nomar Garciaparra

CONTENTS

*T*his shot off the bat of Carlton Fisk in Game 6 of the 1975 World Series remains one of the most dramatic moments in baseball history.

THE HOME RUN

The 1975 World Series between the Cincinnati Reds and Boston Red Sox brought together two teams riding terrible streaks. The Reds had not won a world championship since defeating the Detroit Tigers in the 1940 Fall Classic. The citizens of Boston were even hungrier for a title. Their beloved Sox had not been victorious since just after World War I, back in 1918.

The Big Red Machine

The Cincinnati Reds were clear favorites to take the 1975 World Series. The "Big Red Machine" had won 108 games during the regular season. They proceeded to sweep the Pittsburgh Pirates in three games in the National League Championship Series. The Reds were led by a few Hall of Fame-caliber players, such as catcher Johnny Bench, third baseman Pete Rose, second baseman Joe Morgan, and first baseman Tony Perez. Morgan won the first of his consecutive

National League Most Valuable Player (MVP) awards in 1975. Manager Sparky Anderson had 15-game winners Gary Nolan, Jack Billingham, and Don Gullett heading his pitching staff. In the bullpen, Rawley Eastwick tied for the league lead in saves, with Will McEnaney not far behind.

American League Champs

Carl Yastrzemski had been a mainstay of the Red Sox since 1961. He was joined in 1975 by a pair of power-hitting rookie outfielders—Jim Rice and Fred Lynn. Lynn put together a magnificent season, becoming the first rookie in history to win the MVP award. He hit 21 homers, brought home 105 runs, and finished second in the league in batting, with an average of .331. Rice batted .309, hit 22 homers, and drove in 102 runs. Unfortunately he was hit by a pitch that broke his left hand during the last week of the season, and missed the entire postseason. Behind the plate, the Boston pitching staff was guided by Carlton Fisk. Fisk had been injured in spring training and did not play until June. He came back with a bang, however, hitting .331 over the final seventy-nine games.

When the Red Sox swept the Oakland Athletics in the American League Championship Series (ALCS), it set up a World Series between the two highest-scoring teams in the majors.

The 1975 World Series

The 1975 World Series proved to be one of the most exciting in history. The Red Sox broke on top in

Game 1 behind 18-game winner Luis Tiant. The veteran hurler baffled the Reds in tossing a five-hit, 6–0 shutout. Cincinnati bounced back the next day, scoring a pair of runs in the ninth inning to hand Boston a 3–2 defeat. Game 3 was another nail-biter that Cincinnati again won in its last at-bat. Boston had tied the score on a two-out, two-run home run by Dwight Evans in the ninth inning. The Reds came back to score the winner in the bottom of the 10th inning. The final run was set up by a controversial play that saw Reds outfielder Ed Armbrister apparently commit interference. After bunting the ball in front of the plate, Armbrister hesitated as Red Sox catcher Carlton "Pudge" Fisk charged out from behind the plate. Fisk pushed Armbrister out of his way, retrieved the ball, and then threw it into center field for a two-base error. Boston claimed that Armbrister had interfered, but the umpires allowed the play to stand, and the runner eventually came around to score.

The Red Sox evened the series behind another Tiant victory in Game 4, winning 5–4. When Cincinnati took the next game, however, it put the Sox on the brink of defeat. Boston would have to win Game 6 or go home for the winter.

"Some Kind of Game"

After three days of rain, the two teams took the field at Boston's Fenway Park on the night of October 21. Luis Tiant was making his third start for the Red Sox, while right-hander Gary Nolan took the mound for the visitors. Fred Lynn hit a three-run homer in the first

*C*arlton Fisk urges the ball over the Green Monster after connecting off of Cincinnati's Pat Darcy in the 12th inning of Game 6.

inning to give Boston the lead. The Reds bounced back to score three in the fifth, then followed with two more in the seventh and another in the eighth inning, for a 6–3 advantage. Cincinnati fans could smell victory.

The Red Sox would not be counted out. Pinch hitter Bernie Carbo slugged a three-run homer in Boston's half of the eighth inning, and the score was knotted at six apiece. "I was telling myself not to strike out," reported the lefty swinger. "I was just trying to put the ball in play someplace."[1]

The Red Sox loaded the bases with nobody out in the last of the ninth, but failed to score as left fielder George Foster threw out a runner at the plate. In the top of the 11th, Boston right fielder Dwight Evans made a miraculous catch to rob Joe Morgan of a home run and keep the Sox's hopes alive. A sprawling grab

8

by Fisk of a Johnny Bench foul pop-up highlighted the top half of the 12th.

As Fisk came to bat leading off the bottom half of the inning, the game was already four hours old. "Pudge" took his stance in the batter's box to face Pat Darcy, the eighth Cincinnati pitcher. After taking the first pitch for ball one, the catcher swung at Darcy's next offering and sent it arching far down the left-field line. Fisk moved from the plate, keeping his eye on the ball as it hooked toward the foul pole. He urged the ball fair with all the body language he could gather. When the ball finally cleared the wall in fair territory, Fisk leaped into the air. The Red Sox were victorious, winning what Pete Rose would always would remember as "some kind of game."[2]

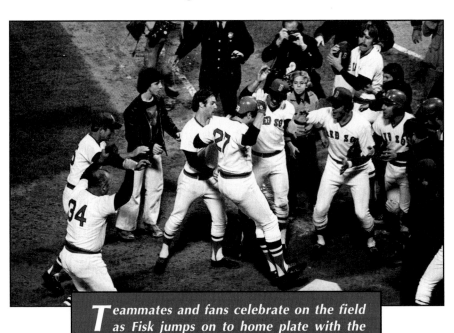

Teammates and fans celebrate on the field as Fisk jumps on to home plate with the winning run.

*F*enway Park originally opened in 1912. This aerial photo was taken in April 1994.

A GRAND TRADITION

When the American League began play in 1901, Boston was one of the original ball clubs in the eight-team league. At various times, the team was called the Americans, Pilgrims, Puritans, Plymouth Rocks, and Somersets. It did not become known as the Red Sox until the 1907 season.

A New Franchise

The first Boston clubs were dominated by slugger Buck Freeman and Hall of Fame pitcher Cy Young. The two veterans led the team to pennants in 1903 and 1904. Over the next few years, owner John Taylor made a series of unpopular deals, and the team's fortunes declined.

New young stars, however, were on their way up, as was a new home field. Fenway Park was completed in time for the opening of the 1912 season. Helping rebuild the offense were Tris Speaker, Harry Hooper, and Duffy Lewis, and a pitching staff led by Smoky

Joe Wood. The Sox won a team record 105 games that year. Wood won 34 himself, while Speaker batted .383. The Red Sox went on to defeat the Giants that fall in an exciting World Series.

The Babe Ruth Years

Led by a young left-handed pitching star by the name of Babe Ruth, Boston won three more world championships: 1915, 1916, and 1918. Ruth compiled a record of 78–40 during that time. He led American League pitchers in earned run average and shutouts in 1916, and in complete games the following season. His hitting, however, attracted even more attention than his hurling. By 1918, he was playing the outfield on days he was not due to pitch. He responded by clouting 11 home runs to tie for the league lead.

Needing to make up for money he had been losing, owner Harry Frazee began to sell his players' contracts to other teams. Many of them went to the Yankees. The Red Sox dropped to sixth place in 1919, despite Ruth's record 29 home runs. That December, Frazee did the unthinkable: He sold Ruth to the New York Yankees for $100,000 and a $350,000 loan. "I was disgusted," outfielder Harry Hooper would recall years later. "The Yankee dynasty of the twenties was three-quarters the Red Sox of a few years before."[1] Boston would finish in no higher than fourth place over the next eighteen years. In recent years, some Red Sox fans have blamed the team's failure to win another championship on a supposed curse dating back to this ill-fated Babe Ruth deal. It is known as the curse of the Bambino.

Owner Tom Yawkey

Tom Yawkey purchased the Sox in 1933. Over the next three years, he made a series of trades for veteran stars. These included Lefty Grove (who, it was said, "could throw a lamb chop past a wolf"),[2] Jimmie Foxx, and Joe Cronin. Boston improved in the standings. The team did not move back into pennant contention, though, until young players such as Ted Williams and Bobby Doerr joined the team. Yawkey's efforts were finally rewarded when the 1946 club won 104 games to take the pennant, but lost the World Series to the St. Louis Cardinals in seven games.

George Herman "Babe" Ruth helped pitch the Red Sox to three championships: 1915, 1916, and 1918. By 1918, he had begun to play the outfield regularly.

Powered by the magnificent Williams, the Red Sox were often in playoff contention over the next dozen years. The New York Yankees, however, won ten pennants over that period of time. The closest the Sox came to another pennant was in 1948. The team finished strongly to end up in a tie for first with Cleveland. Unfortunately, Boston then lost a one-game playoff to the Indians.

The Curse Strikes Again

After another ninth-place finish in 1966, the Sox made a dramatic turnaround in 1967. Led by Carl Yastrzemski, Boston won its first pennant in twenty-one years. Yaz could not work his magic in the World Series, however, as the Cardinals defeated Boston in seven games.

Although they were often in the chase, the Red Sox did not win another pennant until 1975. A core of young players, led by outfielders Jim Rice and Fred Lynn, sparked the team. Lynn was the first player in major-league history to win the Rookie of the Year and MVP awards in the same year. In the World Series, however, the Red Sox suffered yet another seven-game defeat, this time at the hands of the Cincinnati Reds.

A Playoff Defeat

Ahead by seven and a half games in late August, the Red Sox proceeded to blow their lead and fall three and a half games behind the Yankees by mid-September. Incredibly, Boston won twelve of its last fourteen games, including eight in a row, to finish in a tie with New York. In the one-game playoff to determine the division championship, Yankees shortstop Bucky Dent came to the plate in the seventh inning, with two men on and the Red Sox leading, 2–0. He was carrying a bat that teammate Mickey Rivers had given to the batboy. "Give this to Bucky," instructed Rivers. "Tell him there are lots of hits in it. He'll get a home run."[3] Amazingly, the light-hitting Dent did just that. He stroked a pop fly over the left-field wall at Fenway Park to erase Boston's lead. Trailing 5–4 with two outs in the bottom of the ninth and the tying run on third base, the Sox again came up short, as Yastrzemski popped up for the final out.

DENTON T. (CY) YOUNG
CLEVELAND (N) 1890-98
ST. LOUIS (N) 1899-1900
BOSTON (A) 1901-08
CLEVELAND (A) 1909-11
BOSTON (N) 1911
ONLY PITCHER IN FIRST HUNDRED
YEARS OF BASEBALL TO WIN 500 GAMES,
AMONG HIS 511 VICTORIES WERE 3
NO-HIT SHUTOUTS, PITCHED PERFECT
GAME MAY 5, 1904, NO OPPOSING
BATSMAN REACHING FIRST BASE.

*C*y Young is baseball's all-time winningest pitcher, with 511 victories. Today, the best pitcher in each league receives a Cy Young Award.

THE CREAM OF THE CROP

Over the years, many of the biggest stars in the big-leagues have played for the Red Sox. Several of them are now enshrined in the National Baseball Hall of Fame, in Cooperstown, New York.

Cy Young

If a person had to pick one unbreakable major-league record, it would most likely be Cy Young's 511 career wins. Walter Johnson is the only other hurler to have reached 400, and he came up 94 short, with 417. As Young once told a reporter, "I won more games than you ever saw."[1]

Young achieved 192 of those victories during the eight years (1901–08) he spent with Boston. He won more than thirty games in a season five times in his career, including 33 in 1901 and 32 the next year. In 1903, his 28 wins led the team to the American League pennant. The Red Sox defeated the Pirates, five games to three, to take the first modern-day World Series. Young recorded two of those wins.

Young also hurled a pair of no-hitters while pitching for Boston. The first of those was a perfect game against the Philadelphia Athletics in 1904. The second was an 8–0 beauty against New York in 1908. He was elected to Baseball's Hall of Fame in 1937. Less than a year after Young's death in 1955, the Baseball Writers' Association of America established the Cy Young Memorial Award to honor the major leagues' outstanding pitcher each year.

Ted Williams

Theodore Samuel Williams never asked for much. "All I want out of life," he once said, "is that when I walk down the street folks will say, 'There goes the greatest hitter who ever lived.'"[2] By the time he retired following the 1960 season, many people believed he had reached that goal. Despite missing nearly five full seasons due to military service, the "Splendid Splinter" put together an incredible list of accomplishments. These included a career .344 batting average and .634 slugging percentage, two Triple Crowns (1942, 1947), two MVP awards (1946, 1949), and a .406 batting average in 1941. Were it not for Williams's outspoken and often combative attitude toward the media, he undoubtedly would have accumulated even more honors. In his Triple Crown year of 1947, for example, one sportswriter left his name off the MVP ballot altogether. He lost the vote by a single point.

The Boston Red Sox Baseball Team

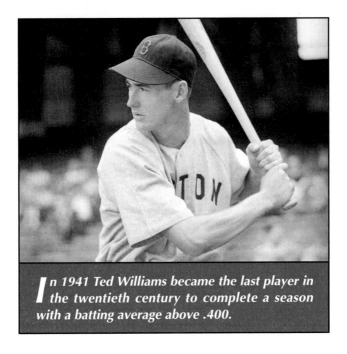

*I*n 1941 Ted Williams became the last player in the twentieth century to complete a season with a batting average above .400.

"Teddy Ballgame" closed out his career in dramatic fashion. In 1960, he hit home run number 521 in his final big-league at-bat. Incredibly, he finished the year with a .316 batting average at the age of forty-two. Williams was voted into the Hall of Fame in 1966. Three years later he returned to baseball, taking over as manager of the lowly Washington Senators. He met this new challenge by leading the franchise to its first winning record.

Carl Yastrzemski

Carl Yastrzemski was a shortstop when he was originally signed by the Red Sox off the Notre Dame campus in 1959. Two years later he took over for Ted Williams in left field. It was a rare case of one Hall of Famer directly succeeding another. Yaz called Fenway Park home for the next twenty-three years. By the time he retired, he had played in more games (3,308) than anyone else in major-league history. In 1984 that record was surpassed by Pete Rose.

Yastrzemski collected 3,419 hits in his distinguished career, and won three batting titles. He learned to play the "Green Monster" at Fenway to perfection and won six Gold Glove awards for fielding excellence. He is best remembered for almost single-handedly leading the Red Sox to the pennant in their "Impossible Dream" season of 1967. He won the American League Triple Crown that year, leading the circuit in batting (.326), home runs (44), and runs batted in (121). He also topped the league in slugging percentage, hits, and runs scored. Yaz continued his storybook year by batting .400, with 3 home runs, in Boston's seven-game World Series loss to the St. Louis Cardinals. For his efforts, he was honored by the baseball sportswriters with the American League MVP award. Yastrzemski's value to the team was later recalled by former teammate George Scott. "Yaz hit 44 homers that year," remembered the big first baseman, "and 43 of them meant something big for the team. It seemed like every time we needed a big play, the man stepped up and got it done."[3]

Nomar Garciaparra

Nomar Garciaparra burst on the big-league scene in 1997. Taking over as Boston's regular shortstop, he proceeded to lead the American League in base hits with 209, while batting .306, hitting 30 home runs, and driving home 98 runs. In doing so, he set a major-league record for most RBIs in a season by a leadoff

The Boston Red Sox Baseball Team

*I*n his first major league season, Nomar Garciaparra led the American League in hits. He was named the 1997 AL Rookie of the Year.

batter. He was recognized for his achievements by being unanimously voted the AL Rookie of the Year.

Garciaparra followed up in 1998 by hitting .323, with 35 homers and 122 runs batted in. He led Boston to the American League Division Series against Cleveland. Although the Red Sox lost, Garciaparra distinguished himself by hitting .333, with 3 homers and an AL Division Series record 11 RBIs. He finished the year second in the voting for the American League MVP. Manager Jimy Williams had nothing but praise for his shortstop. "His enthusiasm, the skills—everything comes to mind with his makeup," said the skipper. "Offensively, his numbers speak for themselves."[4]

The Cream of the Crop

JAMES COLLINS

CONSIDERED BY MANY THE GAME'S
GREATEST THIRD BASEMAN, HE
REVOLUTIONIZED STYLE OF PLAY AT THAT
BAG. LED BOSTON RED SOX TO FIRST
WORLD CHAMPIONSHIP IN 1903. A
CONSISTENT BATTER, HIS DEFENSIVE PLAY
THRILLED FANS OF BOTH MAJOR LEAGUES.

Jimmy Collins managed the Red Sox to victory in the first World Series.

THE VIEW FROM THE TOP

 good manager brings out the best in his players. The Red Sox have been lucky to have several men capable of doing so.

Jimmy Collins

In the 1890s many considered Jimmy Collins of the Boston Braves to be the greatest third baseman of the day. In 1901 he was offered the opportunity to become player-manager of the Boston club in the newly formed American League. He jumped at the chance and led the squad to a second-place finish in the team's first year of existence. The following season, the Pilgrims (as the Red Sox were known) dropped to third place, but they rebounded to take the pennant in each of the next two years. In 1903 they met the Pittsburgh Pirates in the first modern World Series. Trailing three games to one, Collins's men won the next four contests to take the best-of-nine series and become world champions.

23

Boston won again in 1904, but manager John McGraw of the National League pennant–winning New York Giants refused to let his team play in the Series. Earlier that season, McGraw had said, "When we clinch the NL pennant, we'll be champions of the only real major league."[1] The following year, baseball's newly founded ruling body—the National Commission—established rules for postseason competition between the two leagues. Unfortunately for Collins, Boston dropped to fourth place in the standings. He was replaced toward the end of the 1906 season.

Joe Cronin

Joe Cronin was already well on his way to the baseball Hall of Fame by the time he joined the Red Sox in October 1934. He had driven in 100 or more runs in each of his five previous seasons with the Washington Senators while establishing himself as the American League's outstanding shortstop. He was named player-manager of the Senators in 1933, and at age twenty-seven, led them to the pennant that year.

He took over the reins of the Red Sox in 1935, and he remained in that position for a total of thirteen years. His 2,007 games and 1,071 wins are both team records. He retired as a player in 1945, then led the Sox to the AL pennant the following year. In 1948, at age forty-two, he moved into the front office as general manager, taking over as head of the team's baseball operations. Three years after he was named to the Hall of Fame in 1956, he was chosen as president of the

The Boston Red Sox Baseball Team

R ed Sox manager Joe Cronin stops to talk to owner Tom Yawkey (left) and General Manager Eddie Collins (second from left) before a game in October 1946.

American League by the team owners. He was the first former player ever so honored. He held that position through 1973, presiding over the league's expansion from eight teams to ten in 1960, and to twelve in 1969. During Cronin's long career in baseball he became one of the most respected men in the history of the game.

Dick Williams

Never more than a utility player in his thirteen big-league seasons, Dick Williams was more successful as a manager. He directed six different teams over the course of his twenty-one-year career, winning four

*D*ick Williams managed six different teams in his career and led three of them to the World Series, including the Red Sox during their "Impossible Dream" season of 1967.

pennants and two world championships. His first season at the controls was the most memorable.

After the Red Sox finished in ninth place in 1966, Williams was hired to take over the reins the following season. He drove the team hard, stressing preparation and fundamentals. There was no question that he was in charge, and he did not care whether players liked him or not. "You don't have to go out to dinner with these guys," he said. "Just put the names of the best players in the lineup. If they do the job, they play. If they don't, they don't."[2]

Tough but Fair

His methods may have seemed harsh to many, but they proved to be effective. The Red Sox improved their record by twenty games over the previous season's mark. They edged out the Detroit Tigers for the American League pennant by one game, and came within one game of winning the World Series. Williams refused to second-guess his style of managing. "I had no friends on that team," he would later say. "I was sarcastic and belligerent, but I got the most out of the players."[3]

*C*arl Yastrzemski is shown hitting the second of his two home runs in Game 2 of the 1967 World Series against the St. Louis Cardinals.

SEASONS TO REMEMBER

Although they have not won a championship since 1918, the Red Sox still have won more titles than all but four other major-league teams. Their nine appearances in the World Series have featured some of the most unforgettable games in baseball history.

The First World Series

The American League was just three years old when Boston won its first pennant in 1903. The team finished fourteen and a half games ahead of the Athletics, as pitchers Cy Young, Bill Dinneen, and Long Tom Hughes each won at least twenty games. Just prior to the end of the season, Boston owner Henry Killilea and Barney Dreyfuss of the National League-leading Pittsburgh club agreed to a best-of-nine postseason series between the two teams. "The time has come for the National League and the American League to organize a World Series," wrote

Dreyfuss to Killilea. "It is my belief that if our clubs played a series on a best-of-nine basis, we would create great interest in baseball, in our leagues, and in our players."[1]

The underdog Boston squad was defeated by Pittsburgh ace Deacon Phillippe three times in the first four contests. Boston rallied behind Young and Dinneen to even the Series at three games apiece. The two veterans proceeded to shock Pittsburgh by also winning the next two games. Boston's four consecutive victories gave them the championship and established the new league as a true major league.

The Impossible Dream

No one expected much from the Red Sox following their ninth-place finish in 1966. But led by rookie manager Dick Williams and hard-hitting outfielder Carl Yastrzemski, the team put together a dream year in 1967. Outfielder Tony Conigliaro and first baseman George Scott also played important roles, as did pitcher Jim Lonborg. It was Yaz, though, that deserved most of the credit. "It is obviously impossible for one man to win a pennant," wrote Lawrence Ritter and Donald Honig. "And yet if it has ever been done it was done in 1967, and the man who did it was Boston left fielder Carl Yastrzemski."[2]

The year of the "Impossible Dream" came to an end with the Sox losing to the St. Louis Cardinals in the World Series, despite two magnificent pitching efforts by Lonborg. The big right-hander hurled a one-hit shutout in Game 2, and a three-hit victory in

Game 5. Unfortunately for Boston, St. Louis ace Bob Gibson was just as brilliant. With the Series tied at three games apiece, the two aces took the mound for the seventh, and deciding, game. Gibson came out on top, allowing just three hits to win his third game and give the Cardinals the championship.

So Close, Yet So Far

The 1986 Red Sox squad boasted a whole new set of stars. Third baseman Wade Boggs won his third batting title, leading the league with a mark of .357. Designated hitter Don Baylor stroked 31 homers, while left fielder Jim Rice and first baseman Bill Buckner each drove in more than a hundred runs. The pitching staff was led by hard-throwing Roger Clemens. Clemens led the league with 24 victories and an earned run average of 2.48. Included among his wins was a 3–1 win over Seattle in which he set a major-league record by striking out 20 batters. "I watched perfect games by Catfish Hunter and Mike Witt," said manager John McNamara afterward, "but this was the most awesome pitching performance I've ever seen."[3] Clemens was rewarded for his efforts by winning both the Cy Young Award and the AL MVP award.

After winning their division, the Sox played the California Angels in the ALCS. Down three games to one, Boston was one strike away from elimination in Game 5. Dave Henderson's dramatic two-out, two-run homer in the ninth inning brought the team back from the brink of defeat. The Sox went on to win the game in eleven innings. "I looked into their dugout when they

*R*ed Sox third baseman Wade Boggs led the AL in hitting with a .357 average in 1986.

got the second strike on Dave," remembered Clemens, "and they were celebrating. That made it especially nice when we won the way we did."[4] Boston proceeded to take the next two games, to win the series.

Another Heartbreaker

When the Red Sox won the first two games of the 1986 World Series against the New York Mets, it appeared that the long championship famine would finally end. Only one other team had ever lost the first two games at home and come back to win the Series. By the time the teams returned to New York for Game 6, Boston held a three games to two advantage. With Clemens starting, the Sox jumped out to a 3–2 lead, but the Mets tied the score, and the game went into extra innings. Boston scored twice in the top of the 10th. When the first two Mets were retired in the bottom half of the inning, Red Sox fans could taste victory.

That victory, however, was not to be. Three straight singles brought the Mets back within one, and the tying

In 1986, Roger Clemens won both the AL MVP and Cy Young Awards while leading the Red Sox to the World Series against the NL champion New York Mets.

run was on third base. With Mookie Wilson at the plate, Boston pitcher Bob Stanley delivered a wild pitch, and the game was tied. Wilson then proceeded to hit a ground ball that went through first baseman Buckner's legs, and the winning run crossed the plate. "I can't remember the last time I missed a ball like that," Buckner would later say, "but I'll remember that one."[5]

After twice being one strike away from victory, the Red Sox now had to play a deciding Game 7. In Game 7, Boston took a 3–0 lead into the sixth inning before the Mets came back to tie, and eventually win, the game. It was another seven-game Series loss for Boston, and another victory for the "curse of the Bambino."

*M*o Vaughn played for the Red Sox from 1991 to 1998. In 1995, he was named the AL MVP.

TEAM WITH A FUTURE

The Red Sox entered the last decade of the century with high hopes. In 1990 they captured the AL East crown on the final day of the season. Their joy was short-lived, however. The team was swept in three games by the Oakland Athletics in the League Championship Series.

Despite the excellent pitching of Roger Clemens, who won his third Cy Young Award, Boston finished in second place the following year. A change in managers did not turn out to be the answer. Under Butch Hobson, the Sox dropped into the cellar in 1992. They would not win another division title until three years later.

An MVP Season

Kevin Kennedy replaced Hobson in 1995, and the Red Sox responded to his leadership. Boston won the AL East by a seven-game margin over the hated Yankees. First baseman Mo Vaughn tied for the American

League lead in runs batted in with 126, while hitting 39 home runs and batting an even .300. "The Red Sox had a team that no one expected to win," said Vaughn. "And we did. In an old-fashioned style of baseball."[1]

For his achievements, Vaughn was recognized by being named the league's MVP. Boston's hopes for a pennant were short-lived, however. Their season ended with the team being swept in three games by the Cleveland Indians in the AL Division Series.

The New Millennium

The second half of the decade saw many changes in Boston. Superstars Wade Boggs, Roger Clemens, and Mo Vaughn left the team by way of free agency. They were replaced by new rising stars like Nomar Garciaparra, Derek Lowe, Carl Everett, and the magnificent Pedro Martinez. "I know Boston hasn't had a World Series winner since 1918," said Martinez upon signing, "but my goal is to win a championship ring here in Boston."[2] The Sox then handed the managerial reins to former Atlanta Braves coach Jimy Williams. "We think Jimy Williams is an outstanding baseball man," said Boston general manager Dan Duquette. "[Atlanta general manager] John Schuerholz said he was the most prepared coach he had ever seen. Coming from him, that's high praise."[3]

Through it all, the team managed to remain competitive on the field. In 1998 the Sox made another appearance in the League Division Series, this time as the wild-card team. Unfortunately, they were eliminated by Cleveland once again, this time in four games.

The Boston Red Sox Baseball Team

*S*tarting pitcher Pedro Martinez is determined to bring a championship to Boston.

*D*uring the 2000 season, pitcher Derek Lowe established himself as one of the best relievers in the game.

A Great Baseball Town

Boston has been one of the foundations of the American League for nearly a century. Today, Red Sox fans have much to look forward to. A new ballpark looms on the horizon. The names of the players may change, but the level of play is certain to remain competitive. Boston's fans have been loyal to their team through the good times and the bad. The players appreciate the backing they receive, and love representing the city. "There's no other city to which I'd rather go to than Boston," said Jimmie Foxx many years ago. "It's the most understanding baseball town in the country."[4]

STATISTICS

Team Record

The Red Sox History

YEARS	LOCATION	W	L	PCT.	PENNANTS	WORLD SERIES
1901–09	Boston	691	634	.522	1903, 1904	1903
1910–19	Boston	857	624	.579	1912, 1915, 1916, 1918	1912, 1915, 1916, 1918
1920–29	Boston	595	938	.388	None	None
1930–39	Boston	705	815	.464	None	None
1940–49	Boston	854	683	.556	1946	None
1950–59	Boston	814	725	.529	None	None
1960–69	Boston	764	845	.475	1967	None
1970–79	Boston	895	714	.556	1975	None
1980–89	Boston	821	742	.525	1986	None
1990–99	Boston	814	741	.523	None	None
2000–	Boston	85	77	.525	None	None

The Red Sox Today

YEAR	W	L	PCT.	MANAGER	DIVISION FINISH
1990	88	74	.543	Joe Morgan	1
1991	84	78	.519	Joe Morgan	2 (tie)
1992	73	89	.451	Butch Hobson	7
1993	80	82	.494	Butch Hobson	5
1994	54	61	.470	Butch Hobson	4

The Red Sox Today (continued)

YEAR	W	L	PCT.	MANAGER	DIVISION FINISH
1995	86	58	.597	Kevin Kennedy	1
1996	85	77	.525	Kevin Kennedy	3
1997	78	84	.481	Jimy Williams	4
1998	92	70	.568	Jimy Williams	2
1999	94	68	.580	Jimy Williams	2
2000	85	77	.525	Jimy Williams	2

Total History

W	L	PCT.	PENNANTS.	WORLD SERIES
7,895	7,538	.512	10	5

W=Wins   **L**=Losses   **PCT.**=Winning Percentage
PENNANTS= Won League Title   **WORLD SERIES**= Won World Series

Championship Managers

MANAGER	YEARS MANAGED	RECORD	CHAMPIONSHIPS
Jimmy Collins	1901–06	464–389	World Series, 1903
Jake Stahl	1912–13	144–88	World Series, 1912
Bill Carrigan	1913–16, 1927–29	489–500	World Series, 1915, 1916
Ed Barrow	1918–20	213–203	World Series, 1918
Joe Cronin	1935–47	1,071–916	AL Pennant, 1946
Dick Williams	1967–69	260–217	AL Pennant, 1967
Darrell Johnson	1974–76	220–188	AL Pennant, 1975
John McNamara	1985–88	297–273	AL Pennant, 1986

Great Hitters

PLAYER	SEA	YRS	G	AB	R	H	HR	RBI	SB	AVG
				CAREER STATISTICS						
Wade Boggs	1982–92	18	2,440	9,180	1,513	3,010	118	1,014	24	.328
Joe Cronin*	1935–45	20	2,124	7,579	1,233	2,285	170	1,424	87	.301
Dwight Evans	1972–90	20	2,606	8,996	1,470	2,446	385	1,384	78	.272
Jimmie Foxx*	1936–42	20	2,317	8,134	1,751	2,646	534	1,921	88	.325
Nomar Garciaparra	1996–	5	595	2,436	451	812	117	436	58	.333
Jim Rice	1974–89	16	2,089	8,225	1,249	2,452	382	1,451	58	.298
Tris Speaker*	1907–15	22	2,789	10,197	1,882	3,514	117	1,559	433	.345
Mo Vaughn	1991–98	10	1,346	4,966	784	1,479	299	977	30	.298
Ted Williams*	1939–42 1946–60	19	2,292	7,706	1,798	2,654	521	1,839	24	.344
Carl Yastrzemski*	1961–83	23	3,308	11,988	1,816	3,419	452	1,845	168	.285

SEA=Seasons with Red Sox R=Runs Scored SB=Stolen Bases
YRS=Years in the Majors H=Hits AVG=Batting Average
G=Games HR=Home Runs
AB=At-Bats RBI=Runs Batted In
*Member of National Baseball Hall of Fame

Great Pitchers

PLAYER	SEA	YRS	W	L	PCT	ERA	G	SV	IP	K	SH
					CAREER STATISTICS						
Roger Clemens	1984–96	17	260	142	.647	3.07	512	0	3,666.2	3,504	45
Dennis Eckersley	1978–84, 1998	24	197	171	.535	3.50	1,071	390	3,286	2,401	20
Pedro Martinez	1998–	9	125	56	.691	2.68	278	3	1,576.1	1,818	15
Joe Wood	1908–15	11	116	57	.671	2.03	225	11	1,434	989	28
Cy Young*	1901–08	22	511	316	.618	2.63	906	16	7,356	2,796	76

SEA=Seasons with Red Sox PCT=Winning Percentage IP=Innings Pitched
YRS=Years in the Majors ERA=Earned Run Average K=Strikeouts
W=Wins G=Games SH=Shutouts
L=Losses SV=Saves *Member of National Baseball Hall of Fame

The Boston Red Sox Baseball Team

CHAPTER NOTES

Chapter 1. The Home Run

1. Joseph Durso, "Red Sox Win to Tie Series," *The New York Times*, October 22, 1975 (as quoted in *The New York Times Encyclopedia of Sports, Volume 2, Baseball* New York: Arno Press, 1979, p. 179).

2. Bert Randolph Sugar, *Baseball's 50 Greatest Games* (New York: Exeter Books, 1986), p. 28.

Chapter 2. A Grand Tradition

1. Lawrence S. Ritter, *The Glory of Their Times* (New York: Macmillan Company, 1966), p. 151.

2. Bob Chieger, ed. *Voices of Baseball* (New York: New American Library, 1983), p. 167.

3. Bert Randolph Sugar, *Baseball's 50 Greatest Games* (New York: Exeter Books, 1986), p. 110.

Chapter 3. The Cream of the Crop

1. Lee Green, *Sportswit* (New York: Fawcett Crest, 1986), p. 53.

2. Daniel Okrent and Harris Lewine, eds. *The Ultimate Baseball Book* (Boston: Houghton Mifflin Co., 1979), p. 340.

3. Herb Crehan, "Carl Yastrzemski," *Red Sox Magazine*, fifth edition, 1999, p. 51.

4. Seth Livingston, "Nomar Garciaparra—Continually Surprising," *Red Sox Magazine*, fourth edition, 1999, p. 4.

Chapter 4. The View from the Top

1. James Charlton, ed. *The Baseball Chronology* (New York: Macmillan Publishing Co., 1991), p. 140.

2. William B. Mead, *The Inside Game* (Alexandria, Va.: Redefinition Books, 1991), p. 40.

3. Ibid., p. 41.

Chapter 5. Seasons to Remember

1. Paul Adomites, *October's Game* (Alexandria, Va.: Redefinition Books, 1990), p. 79.

2. Lawrence Ritter and Donald Honig, *The Image of Their Greatness* (New York: Crown Publishers, 1979), p. 306.

3. Mike Shatzkin, ed., *The Ballplayers* (New York: William Morrow, 1990), p. 195.

4. John Hinds, "1986: An Unforgettable Season!" *1996 Red Sox Official Scorebook Magazine*, fourth edition, p. 55.

5. Dave Sloan, ed., *The Sporting News Official Baseball Guide–1987* (St. Louis, Mo.: The Sporting News, 1987), p. 216.

Chapter 6. A Team of the Future

1. Steven Krasner, "Mo Vaughn, Humility Personified," *1996 Red Sox Official Scorebook Magazine*, first edition, p. 17.

2. Alberto Vasallo III, "He Is Simply Pedro Martinez," *Red Sox Magazine*, first edition, 1998, p. 7.

3. Glenn Miller, "Jimy Williams Points the Way," *Red Sox Magazine*, first edition, 1997, p. 21.

4. Mark Millikin, "Jimmie Foxx: Double X Was Premier Red Sox Slugger," *Red Sox Magazine*, fourth edition, 1997, p. 11.

GLOSSARY

batter's box—Either of two 6-by-4-foot rectangles marked on either side of home plate within which a batter must stand.

batting average—Hits divided by at-bats.

bullpen—the area of the field where relief pitchers warm up during a game.

bunt—A batted ball that is intended to roll slowly along the ground. It may be used either to try for a base hit or to advance a runner.

Cy Young Award—Award given each year to the outstanding pitcher in each league.

designated hitter—A player designated at the start of a game to bat in place of the pitcher. The DH, who does not play the field, is used only in American League ballparks.

ERA (Earned Run Average)—The average number of earned runs per nine-inning game scored against a pitcher. It is determined by dividing the number of earned runs allowed by the number of innings pitched times nine.

general manager—A club official who is responsible for, among other things, acquiring players and negotiating player contracts.

Gold Glove—Award given to the players voted the best fielders at their positions.

League Championship Series (LCS)—A best-of-seven series that determines the champions of the American and National Leagues.

League Division Series—A best-of-five series that determines the two teams that will meet in the League Championship Series.

pennant—A league championship.

perfect game—A no-hitter in which no batter reaches base.

pinch-hitter—A player sent up to bat in place of another player.

slugging percentage—A measure of a batter's effectiveness at making extra-base hits. It is determined by dividing the total bases reached on safe hits by the number of at-bats.

utility player—A player capable of serving as a substitute at any of several positions.

wild card—The non-division-winning team with the best won-lost record in a league in regular-season play. The wild card team plays, along with the three division winners, in the League Division Series.

FURTHER READING

Adomites, Paul. *October's Game*. Alexandria, Va.: Redefinition Books, 1990.

Carter, Craig, ed. *The Series*. St. Louis, Mo.: The Sporting News Publishing Company, 1988.

Charlton, James, ed. *The Baseball Chronology*. New York: Macmillan Publishing Co.,1991.

Chieger, Bob, ed. *Voices of Baseball*. New York: New American Library, 1983.

Dewey, Donald, and Nicholas Acocella. *Encyclopedia of Major League Baseball Teams*. New York: HarperCollins, 1993.

Green, Lee. *Sportswit*. New York: Fawcett Crest, 1986.

Italia, Bob. *Boston Red Sox*. Minneapolis: ABDO Publishing Co., 1997.

Karst, Gene, and Martin J. Jones, Jr. *Who's Who in Professional Baseball*. New Rochelle, N.Y.: Arlington House, 1973.

Mead, William B. *The Inside Game*. Alexandria, Va.: Redefinition Books, 1991.

Okrent, Daniel, and Harris Lewine, eds. *The Ultimate Baseball Book*. Boston: Houghton Mifflin Co., 1979.

Rambeck, Richard. *Boston Red Sox*. Mankato, Minn.: The Creative Company, 1998.

Ritter, Lawrence S. *The Glory of Their Times*. New York: Macmillan Co., 1966.

Ritter, Lawrence, and Donald Honig. *The Image of Their Greatness*. New York: Crown Publishers, 1979.

Shatzkin, Mike, ed. *The Ballplayers*. New York: William Morrow, 1990.

Smith, Ron, ed. *Official Major League Baseball Fact Book 1999 Edition*. St. Louis, Mo.: The Sporting News, 1999.

Sugar, Bert Randolph. *Baseball's 50 Greatest Games*. New York: Exeter Books, 1986.

Thorn, John, and Pete Palmer, eds. *Total Baseball*, fifth edition. New York: Viking Penguin, 1997.

INDEX

WHERE TO WRITE AND INTERNET SITES

Official Site of Boston Red Sox
http://www.redsox.com

ESPN's Red Sox Page
http://sports.espn.go.com/mlb/
clubhouse?team=bos

**Major League Baseball's
Red Sox Page**
www.majorleaguebaseball.com/u/
baseball/mlb/teams/BOS/index.html

National Baseball Hall of Fame
http://www.baseballhalloffame.org

Boston Red Sox
Fenway Park
4 Yawkey Way
Boston, MA 02215